I0159329

How to Hire Good People and Keep Them

Alex Merturi

.

HOW TO HIRE
GOOD PEOPLE AND
KEEP THEM

ALEX MERTURI

Copyright © 2020 Alex Merturi

All rights reserved. No part of this publication may be reproduced, stored in a retrieval system, or transmitted, in any form or in any means – by electronic, mechanical, photocopying, recording or otherwise – without prior written permission.

ISBN: 978-0-578-68197-9

alexmerturi.com

CONTENTS

THE FOUR KEYS

- ⊞ Hiring
- ⊞ Training
- ⊞ Motivation
- ⊞ Retention

This book is about success in retail. In a nutshell, it's all about finding good people and keeping them and providing a culture that both makes them effective and resonates with your customers.

It all starts with giving the hiring process the attention that it deserves. In my QSR restaurants, 60% of the staff has more than five years of tenure in an industry where the average turnover rate is 132% in hourly employees and 50% in managers.

This book will teach you the core concepts necessary for finding and keeping the best employees. Learn how to find potential employees by doing a full-scale canvas in the right places. Identify the candidates with great potential using the right signs. Make use of continuous interviews to keep staffing levels up.

Understand how to effectively train. It's not about just teaching someone to grill a burger or manage the cash register. It's about creating a culture of satisfaction, as workers become confident in their skills and build an energized team. This positive feeling, the sense workers have of being good at their jobs, will spill over to your customers.

It's also critical to grasp that effective motivation leads to retention. But most managers don't think about motivating effectively—they focus on what's going wrong. The key to effective motivation is praising workers when they do something well—two words of praise are worth one word of blame. Learn other ways of incentivizing employees and a few special ways of reinforcing that motivation.

Finally, retention is based on learning how to listen to your employees and getting to know them. A good relationship with your employees—one that goes just far enough, but not too far— will make an essential difference in your ability to retain them.

It's all about people. This book will give you the people skills to becoming a star retail/ QSR manager, and that leads directly to commercial success.

WHY PEOPLE ARE THE KEY

My career has been dedicated to retailing success in quick service restaurants (QSRs)—in my case, more than 22 years of owning and managing Subway franchises.

Though my experience is with Subway, what I've learned about retailing applies to many other types of businesses. In a nutshell: Creating a healthy culture is the key to hiring and retaining staff. I learned this very early in my career during high school. I tried a few "entry-level" jobs in and around my hometown of Stamford, Connecticut, and I discovered two things. First, no one cared very much if I did a good job or not. Second, I was a body, filling a slot, and if no disasters occurred, no one paid me much attention. At 15, I got a job at my neighborhood Subway sandwich shop as a Sandwich Artist, and things changed. I discovered what it meant to work on a team. I also found that my skills and attitude were crucial to my own success, as well as to that of the restaurant.

People Matter

I realized at an early age that people matter. Developing people and caring about my co-workers made all the difference to my success.

When I was 17, I knew I wanted to own my own business so that I could put these management ideas to work. To achieve this, I started working three jobs at the same time: as a Subway Sandwich Artist, at Domino's Pizza, and as a valet for a very prestigious restaurant in Greenwich, Connecticut. Meanwhile, IBM hired me for a graphic designer role as a high school intern, and I worked there until about the age of 23. I worked hard because I wanted to own my own business. By working these jobs, I had saved enough money to consider buying a local independent pizza place.

I remember seeking advice from the owner at my Subway, Sean Harrington, a great friend and mentor. He simply asked: "Why don't you buy this Subway franchise instead?"

I was shocked. I thought to myself: How could I own a franchise? It's funny, whether you work as a manager or entry-level employee, you never imagine that one day you could own the whole business.

"How much would it cost?" I asked. He told me $165,000. My jaw dropped. To a 23-year-old kid, $165,000 was like $1.6 million. He told me to try to get a loan. So I tried, and, to my great surprise, I was approved. Thinking back on that moment, if I hadn't tried to get that loan, who knows what direction my life would have gone. I made that franchise a success and the eight others that came afterward, mostly because my ideas about keeping great people worked.

So that's why I wrote this book: to help business owners learn how to find and keep great people—in an industry where you're a hero when you keep someone for three months. I want to share the experiences that have made me successful at having one of the lowest turnover rates in the business.

For the first five years of my career as a Subway franchisee, I purchased underperforming stores and sold them for a profit. Yes, I was a Subway flipper. I later became a corporate trainer for Subway headquarters. I gave new franchisees and managers an in-store experience, coaching and training them in every aspect of running a store. Since I began my career, I've had over 2,000 franchisees train in my stores. I'm also an International Keynote Speaker who talks about QSR retailing, and I have spoken to over 10,000 leaders about how to hire, train, motivate, and retain staff in QSR/retail.

I love mentoring. There is no process more satisfying than helping people grow. If you're good at it, you can transfer all the value of your experience to someone who can use it. And this book will show you how.

HIRE

CHAPTER 1

HIRING

1. Culture Is the Key to Success

Let me describe the elements of how I made all these franchises work.

About 90 to 95% of my staff are 'A' employees, meaning that they do everything well, from the basics to making sandwiches to providing great customer service.

What's more, about 60% of my staff have more than five years of tenure. This is in a sector which, in 2019, witnessed 132% turnover in hourly employees and 50% turnover in managers, according to QSR Magazine.[1]

---

1 https://www.qsrmagazine.com/sponsored/how-keep-staff-turnover-disrupting-your-restaurant

I've also had zero unemployment claims in over 10 years. In contrast, retail layoffs have averaged 15.5% in retail over the past five years, according to the Bureau of Labor Statistics.[2]

It's not possible to exaggerate the importance of this kind of success. Building a healthy culture in your retail space is the key that unlocks all the other elements for growing sales and building incredible teams. Not only are workers happy in their jobs, but that feeling resonates with your customers. It's all about the employee and customer experiences.

It makes everyone smile in the community you're located in when someone mentions your business. You can't advertise for success like that, nor can a marketing campaign spread that feeling.

And it all starts with your own attitude toward working with people.

---

2 https://www.bls.gov/news.release/jolts.t20.htm

2. What Retailing Is All About

Let's look at a brief overview of both QSRs and retailing in general. What's the biggest issue in retailing?

The specialized research firm TDn2K puts it this way: Staffing is a matter of survival for QSR restaurants. Meanwhile, the labor pool is shrinking. "Restaurants are competing with each other for talent, and it goes beyond restaurants that look like your restaurant. People don't get up in the morning and say, 'I'm going to look for a job in a QSR restaurant.' Around 56 percent of restaurants say their primary competition for hourly employees comes from within the segment, and 37 percent say it's restaurants across all segments."[3]

Bear in mind that, according to Upserve, hiring and training an hourly employee costs close to $3,500, after factoring in the costs of the entire hiring process.[4]

You will also read that technology trends are changing the retail industry. To some extent,

---

3 https://www.qsrmagazine.com/sponsored/how-keep-staff-turnover-disrupting-your-restaurant
4 https://upserve.com/restaurant-insider/3-common-reasons-restaurant-employee-turnover/, n.d.

this is true in QSR, as we automate payments and ordering processes.

But it's the people in it that make a restaurant a success, and no amount of technology will change this. Think of the retro 'greasy spoon' diners from back in the 50s and 60s. Customers loved those places because of the owners behind the counter, often a family, who made the place feel like home.

Just because a franchise looks like all the other franchises doesn't mean it can't have its own personality. It should feel like a warm place to come back to, and it should become a part of the community around it.

3. How to Hire

First, let's start with the mistakes we make during the hiring process. Ninety percent of small business owners do what's called "desperation hiring."

Most retail managers assume that there is no point in investing time in the hiring process because turnover is so high.

What they don't realize is that turnover is high precisely because they won't invest time and money in the hiring process—a self-fulfilling prophecy and vicious cycle.

They wait until an employee quits or moves on before starting the hiring process. Then, they put out the old 'Help Wanted' sign and hope for the best. When candidates respond, they go through a cursory interviewing process, and, if there are no obvious issues with the candidate, they hire him/her.

This attitude completely misses the point. It also helps to explain the extremely high turnover rate in our business. "Desperation hiring" means making huge mistakes with potential candidates, which that can severely hurt your business.

An employee at the front counter who can't get along with other employees or customers, for example, is like a hate ambassador for you with the community. Rest assured that every person who encounters this employee will go tell their friends what a rotten time they had at your restaurant. And so the word spreads.

Similarly, an employee who can't get the basics right means that one customer after another will get an order that isn't satisfactory. And again, the word spreads around town about how poor the quality is at your restaurant.

Sure, you will likely fire the unhappy employee. But the damage is done. And with "desperation hiring," you're probably going to hire another person who's unfit for the job.

Remember: Desperation hiring is worse than not hiring anyone at all.

Any experienced manager who takes the time to observe the person being interviewed for a job will sometimes get a gut feeling about the candidate—something is wrong. Our gut feeling may be telling us not to hire this person. But we don't listen.

Why not? Because, as a manager, your first priority is to fill the empty staffing slot. So you convince yourself that this might work, and you allow the need to fill a hole in your schedule overrule your good judgment.

We've seen how detrimental the consequences can be.

So how can we prevent desperation hiring? Let's start with proactively looking for employees in the community.

4. Finding Potential Staff Members

When searching for staff, there are many different places to look. For example, consider looking at places of worship or other community-based organizations. It doesn't matter what your religious background is; just go to a place of worship and ask if they know of some people looking for work. Sometimes, places of worship or other community organizations have bulletins where you can post a job. You should also reach out to the local high school guidance counselors in your area.

Always keep a business card with you. Surprisingly, without even trying, you sometimes meet the perfect candidate. Always be looking for potential hires, even when you don't need anybody. Social media can also be a very effective tool to find candidates, for example, by using geotargeting with Instagram and Facebook. Facebook groups are great places to find prospective candidates. There are Facebook groups for just about everything, right in the area where you are based, from Green Bay Packer moms to New York Yankee dads to Little League baseball in a small town in Idaho. Joining and interacting with these groups can help you find candidates. Many of these local groups are quite large, and these are local people who can help you find employees.

Also, when using social media, like Snagajob, Craigslist, monster.com, or any job recruiting websites, make sure you use the keyword 'cashier.' That keyword will give you a large pool of candidates to choose from.

Never put in the description: "Entry-level job. We will train you. Simple operation, very easy to understand." Be careful because you'll get what you ask for. I can only imagine a kid reading that and thinking, "Oh, dream job. I don't have to do anything."

Try this instead: "Do you love to make people smile? Do you like to serve people? Do you want to be part of a growing organization that develops and cares about their employees?"

Different job descriptions attract different people, so it's wise to be very specific about how you describe the position. Make it enticing, make it exciting, and make it specific to attract the kind of people you are looking for.

5. Ask Your Employees

Don't forget about your most valuable resource! Always start by asking your employees if they know anyone looking for work. Good people often know other good people. On the other hand, don't ask a bad employee, a 'C' or 'D,' if they have friends looking for a job.

6. You Won't Find if You Don't Ask

Let me digress just to give an example. Not long ago, I hired a team of roofers to do some work on my house. From the moment they walked in the door, I got a good vibe from them. They seemed eager to do the work and happy about it. And they were easy to talk to.

They did a great job on my roof. There was not a nail left on the ground when they finished; they were clean, great-attitude, high-energy people. I asked them: "Do you guys know anybody looking for work? I'm trying to find a lunch person to work at my restaurant." They gave me the number of a woman named Wendy. I interviewed Wendy, and I liked her right off the bat. I hired her, and she's a rock star who has been with me for five years.

If you don't ask, you won't find it.

7. Making Hiring Work

Hiring is an art!

It should be on a manager's mind every day, regardless of staffing needs.

The first step to making hiring work for you is to think about it when you don't have a hole in your schedule. The trick to hiring is to always be interviewing, regardless of your needs. If you have a full staff, you almost certainly have some C- or D-level employees. This is your chance to replace them. This also creates a pool of quality candidates who can be called on when you need them, but, even more importantly, it allows you to fully engage in the interviewing process, giving it all the time, attention, and resources it requires. Hiring starts when the candidate first walks in the door.

Careful, attentive hiring based on observation, feelings, and the candidate's reactions leads to assurance about who to hire.

Start when the candidate first comes in the door. Don't wait, as most managers do, until all the forms are filled out and the person is waiting for you. You'd be missing an ideal chance to observe how the person responds. When the candidate comes in the door, gauge his/her attitude. Is the candidate eager? Nervous, scared, indifferent? Does the candidate seem happy to be here?

The point is: What's the person like? Earnest, smiling, uptight? Graceful or clumsy?

Can you get all this when a person just comes through the door?

Maybe not, but you can get a lot. And what you get at this point, you can develop further through the interviewing process.

Usually, my interview starts on a Friday at 3:00 p.m. I am out front, sitting in the customer area about 20 minutes before my first interview. I have to be there early enough to capture every part of my hiring process. If I wait until after the candidate comes in and all the forms have been filled out to sit down, I will be missing far too much valuable information.

I think of hiring as a three-step process.

1. Walk in the front door

2. Walk to the interview table (nonverbal cues)

3. Interview

Step 1: Walk in the front door

How someone walks in the door provides information. This is what I pay attention to—if a candidate opens the front door, comes in, and makes eye contact with me or my staff: Do they smile naturally? In the retail business, you need natural smilers working behind the counter. Many great people are not natural smilers. But most customers don't want to see miserable faces behind the counter. So, you pay attention at the start and try to find natural smilers. There was a time when I thought I could teach people how to smile. I said to myself: Even if it kills me, I'm going to teach this person how to smile.

What I learned was that you cannot teach someone how to smile if it's not inherent in them. Smiling is natural. Either you are a smiler or you are not a smiler. So, when a candidate comes in the front door and makes eye contact, check for that natural smile.

Now when they speak to one of your frontline personnel, how do they communicate that they are there for the interview? Do they seem arrogant? Or do they say it in a very nice way that comes across as respectful and kind? How they communicate why they are there tells me a lot about that individual.

Filter Out Nervousness

You shouldn't allow a candidate's nervousness affect your judgment. In fact, part of your skillset as an interviewer should be to 'filter out' nervousness from other qualities in a candidate. Most candidates for QSR jobs are quite young, often in their mid- to late teens. They have little to no interviewing experience and are nervous. You can ignore that and evaluate the more important aspects of their character instead.

Character is what we're interested in assessing. We want to know if this person has the energy and the responsiveness to be a good worker.

Step 2: Walk to the interview table

After the candidate arrives for the interview and greets a member of my staff, I'll then approach them with a pen and an application that they must fill out by hand. Like most retailers, we provide an online application that the candidate has already filled out. But I want to get their reaction to filling out a second application. This is important because I want to see the candidate's reaction. If the reaction is: "I've already done this," it tells me that they just want to make this as quick and easy as possible. If they have a positive reaction, it tells me that the candidate is willing to take that extra step. Now, I ask them to go to my interview table, which is on the other side of the room. I pay attention to how the individual walks to the table. How somebody walks tells me a tremendous amount about them. Does it take them a few seconds longer than most people to get to the interview table, or do they get to the interview table rapidly? How a person walks tells me a lot about their energy level. Most slow walkers don't have much energy; most fast walkers have quite a lot. I also pay attention to how a person pulls up a chair to sit down. Have you ever seen someone take an eternity to pull up a chair and sit down? That's a low-energy individual. A person with energy moves rapidly to the table, quickly pulls up a chair, sits down, and starts writing.

Energy is everything in our business and in any other business. I truly believe that a person with average intelligence and high-energy will outperform a brilliant guy with low energy. So, when you're analyzing prospective employees, pay attention to their energy level. Have you ever talked to an employee for 15 minutes, and when you got into your vehicle, you're exhausted because they drained the energy out of you? Either you give energy or you take energy, and I'm on a mission to find people who give and radiate energy.

Now, pay attention as they fill out the application. Are they using their phone? Or are they focused on finishing the application? This indicator of attitude matters too. If the manager misses Step 1 and Step 2, then the interviewing process is botched, with too many missed opportunities.

Step 3: Interview

During the actual interview, the first question that I ask is: "Tell me about yourself?" While the candidate is talking, I'm not focusing much on what they're saying. I watch for their nonverbal cues. How are they sitting? How are they communicating with me? Are they looking me in the eye when they talk to me? Your old man probably told you that a firm handshake and eye contact are important—well, that's still true today. This is the moment to listen to what your gut is telling you about the candidate or to pay attention to that voice in your head, that gut feeling which is right about 99% of the time.

Listen to your gut feelings

In retail, it's often hard to let your feelings be your guide. You have to fill a slot, and, by some miracle, a person comes in wanting to work the exact hours you need to be filled.

You interview that person, and the voice in your head says, "Don't do it! Don't hire this person!" But logic tells you not to listen because you need the slot filled. So, you suppress your feelings, and you make the hire. And it's a disaster, of course.

I do just the opposite. I pay attention to nonverbal cues and my gut feelings first. Then I focus on the questions I want to ask in the interview.

In most states, there are legal restrictions on what questions you may ask, so be aware of the questions you ask and how you ask them.

One of the most important questions I ask is, "Tell me about something you've done in your life that you're proud of?"

It doesn't matter what it is—it can be about videogames or something they did in school—I just want to hear the person talk about it, be excited about it. I pay very close attention to the level of enthusiasm as the person tells the story.

Can you imagine someone telling you something that they have done that they're excited about, and he/she doesn't smile when talking? Nor do the storyteller's eyelids even open up just a little bit more when telling you about it?

That's a problem in my book. If you're telling me about something you're proud of, you should show excitement and enthusiasm during the whole story.

8. Interviewing Is a Misnomer

I wish I could come up with another name for this process besides 'interviewing.' I don't like this word because the more formal you make an interview, the further from the truth you're going to be. An interview should be more of a conversation than a formal interview, and it's up to the manager to make that happen.

To the candidate, the interviewer is not even a real person. The exchange is not a real conversation. What you have to do as an interviewer is to let your guard down, make yourself real, and connect with the person you are interviewing. Connecting means that you need to be vulnerable and share a little about who you are, what your company is about, and what you believe in.

When I make the conversation real and per-sonal, like one I might have with a colleague or friend, then I expect the candidate to show some excitement or passion about something they claim to care about. You may say, "I love sleeping," but if you say it with passion and excitement, I'm likely to hire you. If a per-son is excited or passionate about something in his/her life, you can leverage that energy to help grow your business. But a person with no passion and enthusiasm will do nothing but drain every ounce of energy in your retail space.

Remember, you must connect with them to get the truth, so have a good long conversation—the more you talk to the person, the easier it will be for your subconscious to kick in and point you in the right direction.

See if the person is a team player. Kids that play sports tend to be disciplined, work well with others, and manage their time well.

Go with your gut—don't wait!

You'll read about the importance of the second interview in books about hiring. Don't believe a word of it.

Once a girl came in for an interview who was the captain of the cheerleading team. When I sat down with her, everything in my head and in my subconscious told me she's fantastic, she has great energy, she shows great leadership qualities, hire her!

But the book told me to wait until the second interview. So, I held off. I waited for two days. Then, I called her up for the second interview, and, guess what—she had found another job.

I immediately took the book that I'd read and threw it in my fireplace.

Remember, in retail, we're not always looking for experienced people, especially in entry-level jobs. The natural smiler, the high-energy person, the good person, that's a hire. After the interview is over, I usually tell the candidate that we have other interviews and we'll call you for the next step if we decide to move forward. Right before the candidate leaves, I ask them to meet some of my existing staff. All I provide is an introduction. I will say: "Hi, this is Mike Rogers. Please meet Stacy Kohl, who is a Sandwich Artist for the company." Stacy says hi. Mike says hi, and they get a quick little vibe. Mike then leaves (and I watch his energy as he goes to the door). I then ask Stacy a simple question: "Just on your gut feeling, I want you to rank this individual from a one to 10. But you're not allowed to use seven." (Seven is a safe number because it doesn't give me any insight on how that employee feels about the candidate.) Perhaps the employee says eight, meaning they felt good about that individual. If the employee says six, that means they weren't crazy about that individual. This process has the additional advantage of making my staff feel like they are part of the hiring process. If I hire a candidate who was given a rating of eight by a staff member, then the staff member feels empowered, like an important decision-maker. Besides, they'll be the ones to work with the new employee. Being part of the hiring process feeds directly into team building.

I also look carefully at a candidate's job history. If a candidate hasn't held a job for more than eight months, if he/she had a job two months here, five months there, and again two months somewhere else, then that individual may be a job hopper, and it's best not to waste time with a job hopper. If a candidate lists "not enough hours" as a reason for leaving a job, I also see that as a red flag because I know 'A' employees are usually given as many hours as they want.

Also, when I'm reviewing the application, I pay attention to where they've worked before. But I do this in a unique way. Normally, a manager calls references. But, over the phone, you can only ask one question legally: "Would you re-hire this person again?" The answer to that question doesn't help you because most references will say 'yes' just to avoid trouble. Instead, I visit references. Call me crazy, but you have to remember that hiring a new worker is critically important to your success, so sometimes you have to do the extra work to find great people. I put my retail uniform on. I walk into the place that the candidate used to work, order food or coffee, and strike up a conversation with the employees in the back. When they see me with my uniform, they treat me like a colleague. Then I say: "You know, guys, how hard it is to find good help. Have you ever heard of a kid named Mike Rogers? He came in looking for a job."

When I say Mike's name, I focus on their eyes, just like a hawk looking at its prey. You can tell a lot by a person's reaction, and when a person connects with you, they will really let you know how they feel.

So, I get the truth about a person's job history in this way. Armed with all this forethought and these procedures, you can make hiring a success.

CHAPTER SUMMARY

Staffing is a matter of survival for QSR restaurants. The costs of hiring and training a new employee are about $3,500 per person, far more than a franchise can absorb.

But finding and hiring a productive employee is an art—one that you can learn. Learn how to find good candidates in the community around you by asking other good employees and people you respect. Learn to observe new job candidates from the very start to accurately gauge their potential. It's a three-step process: walk in the front door, walk to the interview table, and interview.

Learn how to make the job interview work for you.

TRAIN

CHAPTER 2

TRAINING

1. Why Retailers Fail at Training

I t would, of course, be a shame to hire great people and then to see them fail because of poor training.

Yet, a lack of robust training is practically a byword of the retailing industry—although it's at its worst in QSR.

A recent article in *Retail Dive* shows that, while retailers do invest in training, they don't get much bang for their buck in terms of performance as a result.[5] A fact that employees don't appreciate. Average turnover in retail?

---

5 https://www.retaildive.com/news/most-retail-employees-receive-no-real-training/517522/, n.d.

Sixty percent, according to the National Association of Retailers.[6] As for QSR, a well-known retailing website recently did a survey of how frequently brands train their employees to deal with abusive customers.[7] The answer: not much. Most of the time, it's just a short bit in the training manual. Allowing abusive customers to leave even more pissed off to tell everyone about their rotten experience at your restaurant is a recipe for business disaster. If you're lucky, they don't put it on Twitter or other social media platforms.

As Zeynep Ton, an associate professor of operations management at the MIT Sloan School of Management, explains that retailers of all kinds simply did not bother with training employees who, they assumed, would not be around long. "Mediocrity has been considered sufficient for a long time. Retailers are so focused on minimizing labor costs. It makes for bad jobs for employees and bad service for customers."[8]

_____

6 https://www.qsrmagazine.com/mike-ganino-crafting-culture/4-ways-build-better-restaurant-cul-ture-through-training
7 https://www.qsrmagazine.com/mike-ganino-crafting-culture/4-ways-build-better-restaurant-cul-ture-through-training, n.d.
8 https://www.retaildive.com/news/most-retail-em-ployees-receive-no-real-training/517522/, n.d.

2. Training Is a Golden Opportunity to Build Culture

Most QSR managers see training as a necessary evil—a distraction that takes away time from doing the actual job.

What they don't see is that training provides a golden opportunity to build your team's culture—not just for the new hire but for the entire team.

And the good vibrations that you bring in through these training sessions will rack up sales, as customers react to the warm feeling they get from your restaurant.

First of all, it's necessary to understand what training is really about. It's not just about teaching someone to grill a burger or put together a sandwich. It's a chance to create the right attitude in the new hire, one that will say, day after day on the job, "I feel good. I feel like I know what I'm doing. I feel like my teammates appreciate me." When your staff feels like this, they work well together and your customers notice.

Training is also not a skills test. You don't give out grades. Bear in mind that you will always have some employees who can do every-thing and do it well—'A' level workers—and others who aren't as skilled but who are great at part of the job and who fit in really well on the team—the 'B' players.

You always want to have a mix of 'A' and 'B' players. You can't just have a fastball; you have to have a curveball too—it's the mix that matters.

The 'C' players who don't add value are those who you'll have to replace eventually. But any worker who doesn't maintain the culture must go. Immediately.

To make this clearer, let me give you an example: Not long ago, I had an A+-level worker, from an operations perspective. She made sure things ran perfectly, from following instructions to executing operational tasks to maintaining brand standards. But interpersonally, she was an F—she couldn't get along with any of her co-workers. So, she's building my business from an operations perspective on the one hand but killing my culture on the other. Nobody wanted to work with her. Ultimately, customers will sense that something isn't right when she is around working with others. A business without a strong culture will eventually crumble, even if you are operationally excellent. Your foundation is the culture, and you have to pay close attention to that first. A strong foundation in any business will help it grow. So, I had to make the tough decision to let her go.

This is never an easy decision to make, and it's always tempting to postpone it with the justification, 'She shows up for work, and she's really good at her job.'

Don't let yourself settle for this. She's not helping you to build your culture. She's actually hurting your business. So, suck it up and let her go. Making those tough decisions can help you reinvent yourself or force you to work on things that can make your business better.

3. How to Train Effectively

Effective training involves baby steps. You don't bombard the new hire with too much information so that they feel overwhelmed. You also don't teach too many tasks at once. One basic key to training is that the trainee must feel successful, like they've accomplished something. Build that feeling from the start, and then repeat that operation again and again.

Training should start with the basics. How do you clean a table? How do you clean the bathroom? Explain these things clearly, and then show the trainee how important these basics are for customers. Even better, model it yourself to show that nobody is above doing the most basic or menial of jobs.

Many managers make the mistake of skipping the basics, thinking that getting to the money-making aspects of the job, like preparing products and selling them to customers, is more important.

This ignores a few basic facts about human nature. If an employee doesn't have to clean toilets in their first weeks of work, when the time comes to do the job, they'll feel like it's not part of the job description. Why should they have to clean the toilet? When forced to do the job, resentment builds.

This doesn't happen if you make this their first experience at work. Set a precedent in the beginning.

4. Gamification

As I mentioned earlier, successful training involves the whole team, not just the new hire. Gamification offers a way to do this, a way to make training both fun and fulfilling for everyone.

Suppose a certain amount of meat must be weighed out before making a sandwich. Bring the whole team together, go to the back room, and then run a contest in which each team member tries to get as close to the correct weight of meat or veggies as possible before putting it on the scale. Offer a small gift certificate or a few dollars as a prize.

Competitions like this bring the team together. And it reminds them of how important it is to measure quantities carefully—even skilled employees need some retraining from time to time. If you're not training all the time, employees lose calibration.

The new hire enjoys the game and is eager to learn the rest of what they need to know.

5. Use of Video

For further training, I make extensive use of videos. I produce them myself on WhatsApp.

Using my iPhone, I hit record, and I have employees build the new formula or sandwich while I narrate. The employees in the video feel like stars—great positive reinforcement. The other employees get the training they need.

This also offers several advantages. First, you can share the videos among employees with just a click. Then, employees can play them over and over again until they feel they have learned what they need. And the young people who work in retail generally prefer video to text and other sources—it's easily their favorite medium.

Video is very useful and successful as a training medium and results in more effective training for many. The trick, however, is not to make the videos too long, never more than two minutes. A longer video just strains attention spans and fails to get the message across.

So, leave out the introduction, the history, and all the other extras. Get right to the point. If employees have questions after watching the video several times, encourage them to ask and you can answer them. Their questions will show how they are thinking about and engaging with your message, and you should treat questions as a positive response. Training is an important piece of employee retention as well. It often happens that you invest the time to train a person for a month, and they quit. If this happens, analyze why you think that individual left. Was it because too much information was given in a short amount of time and training became stressful? We have to remember that this could happen to any of us.

I usually blame myself when someone quits. I think about what I might have done wrong. Also, remember that in some situations, you might not be the problem; they just left for personal reasons. Evaluate every time an employee leaves to make sure you're not missing something on your end. In your QSR business, begin with a simple step to build your new employee's confidence. This is the only way you can train people properly, by building confidence at every step and ensuring they've mastered that step before they move on to the next one. Managers sometimes rush to delegate more and more work to offload some of their own workloads. But paying attention to this detail can help you retain and train people more effectively. As a general manager or owner, you should always be the one to do the initial training for the first three hours. The reason for this is to get a sense of whether the candidate is willing to put in effort and energy and do the job correctly. This is also an opportunity to set expectations for the new hire and ensure they're being trained how you want them to be trained. If you have been in retail awhile, you know if you've made a good hire after watching someone work for three hours. You either say, "Yes, this was a good hire," or "Why did I hire this person?!" If you don't think they are a good fit for the job description, you can let them go after their shift or tell them they are on a probation period and you'll get back to them about their next shift. Doing this doesn't break their spirit, but it gives you more options.

Finally, always pair a new employee with an 'A' employee, at least for the first two-three weeks of training. Pairing a new employee with a 'C' employee will only create another 'C' employee.

CHAPTER SUMMARY

Training offers a golden opportunity to integrate a new employee into the healthy culture you have already created. But most managers see training as a distraction. They are wrong: Teaching the worker the necessary skills and inculcating the right attitude will be extremely worthwhile as the care and good feeling in the restaurant create a friendly atmosphere that will draw in customers.

Training, if it's done properly, is the best possible investment in your business. Make the whole team part of training with gamification and incentives, and use short 2 minutes or less videos to ensure that your employees understand the right way to do things.

MOTIVATE

CHAPTER 3
MOTIVATION

As we've seen, retention is critical in making any retail business profitable. In my experience, effective motivation leads to retention—which is why I have employees that have been with me for 10 years or more.

But effective motivation isn't about things like pay or promotions. A study by software maker 7shifts of 2000 QSR workers showed that more than 40% said that the key factor in job satisfaction is that their managers and co-workers make them happy at work. One manager said: "I think overall, to retain employees is to not have a transaction of 'I pay you, you work for me' but a transaction of shared values and respect. The leading cause of employee loss is management's leadership."[9]

9 https://www.qsrmagazine.com/exclusives/
why-good-employees-quit-restaurants, n.d.

Know Your People

When I had about 50 or 60 employees, I knew all of them. Understand who they are, where they come from, their background, and what words they use. This is really important to motivate: You can't "blanket" your leadership style and use one word to motivate everyone. You have to use the right word for each person. The only way you'll understand that individual is by getting to know who they are.

Now, I'm not a fan of taking staff out on Friday nights to have drinks and party together. But I am a big fan of knowing who they are. What is their background? Where do they go to school? What interests them? What sports do they play?

Knowing these things enables me to use just the right language to connect with them. When you're motivating people, you have to use the art of language—and you can't be lazy about it. If this person likes baseball, start talking in baseball terms so they pay attention and understand you perfectly.

Many managers, when trying to motivate people, use 'blanket' statements, meaning they have one way of delivering a message and think that it's going to fire on all cylinders and motivate or teach the entire staff. That's not how it works. You need to 'speak the dialect' of each person, based on their background.

This is why hiring a best friend or family member can be unbeatable because you share the same language and understanding. But it's also a gamble. The relationship you have can easily go sour, and then you have a disaster because you can't just fire the person, either from the job or from your life. On the other hand, you have the ability to easily communicate with that person, and often they become star employees. If you've ever hired family or a best friend, you know that when it works, it's unbeatable.

With your staff, in general, you need mutual respect. You cannot be too gregarious, too forward. There's a mutual line that you and your staff should never cross.

Still, the idea is to get as close to the line as you can without ever touching it. Then, you will be the most impactful.

The Lead Employee Should Also Be an 'A' Employee

It's also critical that you're careful about how you assign roles in your restaurant. For example, if employees are closing the restaurant, they are supposed to go through a checklist. Employee 1 and Employee 2 closed the store. You come in the next morning and find a mess. The closing procedures weren't followed, things aren't clean, and they didn't put all the things away that they were supposed to.

What happened? Employee 1 is usually a rock star employee, but she's just not a leader. And you have Employee 2, who has leadership qualities but is not too swift with operations. The combination doesn't work; one drags down the other. Employee 2 acted as the (ineffective) leader, but he led Employee 1 to be careless about following the closing procedures, even though she is usually a superb operations person.

It's important to know who the effective leaders are among your staff and understand that even a D-level person could be very effective as a leader—they just may not lead down the path you want them to. That's why you should always have an effective 'A-' or

'B'-level leader at a minimum on shift. That will provide consistent closings and openings of the restaurant because you have effective leaders and star operations people working together. Or, combine an 'A' employee with a 'C' employee, but make sure the 'A' employee is a leader to help bring the other up to a higher level.

Leading With Praise:
Two Positives for Every Negative Word

People really need praise. It makes an enormous difference. For every negative word, you say to an employee, you need to say two additional positive words. This is a rule I insist on with all of my staff and adhere to it myself as well.

It's far too easy to focus on someone's faults and to forget about the praising part. Of course, you can only deal with problems by pointing out what's wrong—I understand that. But you have to remember that constant fault-finding is very demoralizing to an employee.

So, for every negative word, I'm going to find two positive ones that will elevate the employee, making him feel good. That employee needs to understand that he's not hopelessly incompetent but does do a good job some of the time.

This is really important: As I've gone across the U.S. and Canada and spoken in 40 different territories to more than 10,000 leaders, it has become clear that praising just does not come naturally to a lot of people. I get it; we all grew up differently and had different experiences and values. I certainly didn't grow up being praised every minute as a child. I had to learn how to do it for others. In the beginning, it was incredibly uncomfortable to praise someone for how well they did. I was out of my element. As I traveled across the country, I realized that there are so many people who are the same.

Too many leaders make the mistake of assuming that giving praise is a sign of weakness. Or they worry that praising will make an employee feel like they are irreplaceable. Or even worse it will make him/her ask for a raise. That's a rotten mentality.

You're trying to lift the spirits of your team to get them to perform at a high level to create a culture based on good performance, so that means praising when praise is due. Sometimes, it means praising even if it's not really due, for the sake of the greater goal.

Here's the thing about praise: I don't care who you are in this world. There are people out there who will work for somebody, make a ton of money, and be miserable. But there are also people who make less money and actually feel good at their workplace. Most people will gladly choose the latter. Feeling rotten all the time just isn't worth it.

The proof: In the UK, one-third of workers who leave their jobs say that they did so because they didn't feel good or happy at their workplace. They blame poor corporate culture because that matters a lot, and money can't necessarily compensate for it.[10]

As I said, language matters. Whenever we're talking about a mistake an employee makes, I use the pronoun "we" and not "you." I put myself in there with them, rather than pointing the finger of blame at the person. They're part of my team, and they're under my leadership, which means that when they make a mistake, I'm involved because of how I trained them or how I've led them.

That's why I don't say "you did this" or "you did that," which is just demoralizing. Using the word "we," as in "we have to work on together," is a different and much more successful strategy.

Praising must also be done attentively. There are two forms of praise. One is flattery, which is a waste of time because it doesn't have any meaning to the person you are praising. And the other is real praise that is sincere, comes from the heart, and is based on reality.

---

10 https://www.uktech.news/news/a-third-of-uk-workers-leave-their-jobs-due-to-poor-company-culture-20180412

You have to understand the difference if you want to motivate your workers effectively. Just saying "good job" isn't valuable. People can always tell when you are insincere. You have to read your people and make sure they take what you're saying the right way.

When I first started praising my staff, they were a bit shocked. "Did he mean it?" was the reaction because they were not used to receiving praise for anything. But I kept it up. And as I persevered, people began to show appreciation not only for the praise itself, but also for the positive culture and environment we created through this practice. This is how you create a culture in which people want to work for you.

And because I focus on them, on building their confidence, on creating a positive culture, it starts to resonate through the entire organization. The staff starts to work together to build team relationships that are similar to family relationships. And this retains employees for years and goes right to the customers, who get a good feeling when they walk into one of my restaurants.

Setting the Bar High

Setting the bar high to achieve excellent performance is another aspect of a successful culture. Set the bar high, but expect the team to be a few notches below the bar most of the time. That's fine—it gives your team something to work towards. Constantly push the team to reach the bar you've set, but accept that they may not always reach it. If you get that level of performance, you are doing just fine. Find ways to motivate, reward, and teach them to achieve greater things.

It's difficult for a owners to understand that his employees come before the customers. I actually tell my employees that. Why? Because we create the environment in the restaurant together. That's a happy environment, a good place to work in. And this naturally channels to the customer with out even trying. I actually have customers come into my restaurant and tell me that our place is much more comfortable than other stores.

Another interesting aspect of this culture: When you hire new people and they don't fit the culture, the staff makes it clear that they don't fit in. The staff works to preserve the positive environment in the restaurant by rejecting people who might threaten that feeling.

Contests and Games

We keep this atmosphere up with incentive programs that include contests and games. This is a very effective motivator if it is used properly.

Let me give the example of the "cookie challenge." Who can sell the most cookies from a single restaurant in a given month? Whoever sells the most cookies wins a $25 gift card. This is just one example of an infinite variety of games and contests that you can run to keep the morale high among your staff.

To make these kinds of contests most effective, you have to run them like a horse race. Every day you make an announcement about who's in the lead, so the suspense builds. The workers in the lead see how close they are to winning, and they're motivated to do more. I use WhatsApp, which is a mobile phone app that most workers in the age group I employ all use (if they don't have it already, I get them to install it during training). I post who is in the lead every day on WhatsApp to keep up the level of excitement. If you only announce the beginning of the contest and then wait a week, or until the end, people will stop caring. And that means you won't get the incentivization you are seeking. This kind of daily communication is very important. There are, of course, many other apps you could use. The most important thing is the daily posting of the leader and who's in second or third in the contest.

At the end of the month, in this example, we really racked up the cookie sales. But even more importantly, the team had a lot of fun making those sales. The competition made them closer as a group, between the night shift and day shift. That's a very effective motivator, and that's the bigger picture.

Learn How to Listen

Yet another key factor in motivating your staff is knowing how to listen.

Here's an example from one of my employees who's been with me for 13 years. This woman is now a manager, and she does a great job of taking care of one of my stores. But, every so often, this woman needs to vent and needs me to listen to what's going on in her life. It's actually a key point in motivating her; she appreciates it and works harder for me as a result.

Many managers make the mistake of ignoring this kind of prompt from their employees. They come into the shop, the employee starts talking, and then they say, "No, I don't have time to listen to you today. I'm sorry, I've got to go."

This is a huge motivation mistake as a leader. It builds resentment. It hurts feelings. And it makes that high-performing employee you value stop caring about the job she does.

You, as a leader, have to put in 15 minutes of your time to listen. It shows you care and that the person matters. Just by listening, you can get a week of top performance from the employee.

Monitoring Integrates With Praising

To gauge employee performance, I monitor using video cameras. The employees are aware that I do this. It certainly enables me to find out if something is going wrong, and then I bring it to the attention of the employee, using the "we made a mistake" approach discussed above.

But I also make a point of praising employees when I see them doing something really well on the monitors. If I see a worker providing great service to a customer or stocking shelves efficiently, I make sure to provide positive feedback.

In this way, monitoring is not seen as strictly a way to keep an eye on employees. It also reinforces the atmosphere of teamwork and the culture we've built up.

You Have to Connect

Have you ever met a person that causes you to say to yourself, "This is a really smart individual." But you see that he just can't connect with others because he just doesn't know how. (It's like Sheldon on *The Big Bang Theory* if readers can remember that show.) This person really can't connect with the staff or communicate well with them, and performance levels are low as a consequence. And, no matter how brilliant a retail businessperson is, if they can't make that connection, their team member will not stay. It's that simple.

The best leaders in the world can connect with everybody on all levels by finding common ground, building trust, and communicating effectively. The sky's the limit when you can do that.

CHAPTER SUMMARY

Statistics show that one-third of workers leave their jobs because they don't feel happy at work. This explains why successful employee motivation depends on creating a culture of positive feelings. To do this, one has to connect with employees and listen carefully to them. Monitor their work and praise them whenever possible; when something is wrong, give them two positives for every negative, and make positive and encouraging instructions to change. However, it's important to set the bar high for all your workers. Using contests and games as motivation can be very effective in keeping both performance and morale high. Remember to post updates on who's in the lead daily when doing contests. That will make the difference in keeping staff engaged with incentive programs.

RETAIN

CHAPTER 4

RETENTION

Retention is a hot issue in the QSR industry. "The classic strategy with regard to retaining workers was to standardize and 'routinize' jobs, taking the skill out of them," explains Rosemary Batt, chair of HR Studies and International & Comparative Labor at the Cornell School of Industrial Labor Relations. This strategy was intended to create turnover-proof jobs. If you lose someone, it's not a real cost, because they are so easily replaceable."[11]

---

11 https://www.cnbc.com/2019/08/29/fast-food-restaurants-in-america-are-losing-100percent-of-workers-every-year.html, n.d.

But today, the cost of retention has become too high for retailers to absorb easily. With turnover rates estimated at over 130% on average, the cost of retention is estimated at about $2,000 per worker.[12]

There is talk of using robots, of providing all kinds of incentives, and any number of other solutions, but I find that there are much simpler and more cost-effective ways to keep my employees.

---

12 https://www.cnbc.com/2019/08/29/fast-food-restaurants-in-america-are-losing-100percent-of-workers-every-year.html, n.d.

The Attitude of the Owner

When I speak about QSR management, I sometimes get up in front of a hall filled with 500+ people. To discuss retention, I say: "Let me ask you all a question. Dig deep into yourselves and tell me the truth. When you walk into your business in the morning, do your employees look at your face to see what mood you're in? Are you happy? Are you angry? Are you smiling? Are you upset?" Some managers nod in agreement.

If your employees are looking at you to see what mood you're in, then you're not an effective leader because they've learned that your mood determines their day. It's really important to consider how you look as you walk into your restaurant. Be aware of what you are projecting emotionally.

We, as leaders, all have our moods, our ups and downs. But, to be an effective leader, it's not up to me to project my mood onto my employees. Just because you may feel bad, there's no reason why your employees should have to worry about it.

Let's say, for example, It snowed yesterday, and my sales were $200 for the entire day (a very low figure for my restaurants). This makes me angry, and when I walk in the door, I show how angry I am. This then makes my staff agitated.

There's a need to understand self-awareness in all this. It's not an easy concept to communicate, however. Put simply, if you're a leader who has mood shifts, meaning that your highs and lows are obvious to your staff, you will have a very difficult time retaining employees.

I have my moods just like everyone else. We all have personal problems. But, and I cannot emphasize this enough, IT'S NOT UP TO MY TEAM TO WORRY ABOUT MY PERSONAL PROBLEMS.

As a leader, I have to worry about my employees, sometimes even about their personal issues. That's part of being a leader.

But they should not have to worry about me.

I signed up for this. I chose this life. This means I have to man up, or woman up, straighten my back, and look good for my team.

So what that it snowed yesterday? I only made $200, I'm ready to blow a gasket, but when I walk through that door in the morning, I look as serene as a Zen master. And that reassures my team, and they perform well.

They have to know that I'm good. And, that way, I know they will be good.

Now, many QSR brands are franchisee-owned. Take Wendy's as an example. They have a "4 for $4" special: You get a burger or sandwich, French fries, chicken nuggets, and a drink for that money. Some franchise owners aren't happy about that. But let's say I'm one of those franchisee owners or a manager at a Wendy's.

I'm in the store, and I open up my marketing kit right in front of my staff, see this deal, and I'm angry because I don't make much money on this promotion. And I raise it up in the air and yell, "This company doesn't want me to make any money!" What does this accomplish? The team will start thinking, "We're in trouble. Am I going to have a job next week?"

You don't show agitation in front of your team. Customer service and the relationship among team members are what's important. And all this will decay if your team hears you grumbling or sees you agitated.

My team doesn't have to worry about my battles with corporate—that's my worry. You don't say (or indicate) to your team, "You have to make me money."

They have all kinds of responsibilities: operations, processes, managing customers. They shouldn't have to worry about the relationship between corporate and me. Those are issues that I have to fight about with corporate; I don't fight those issues with my employees. They have no hand in decision-making and nothing to do with what the national price promotion is.

As an owner, my behavior channels through my employees. You have to be self-aware and understand how you're being perceived by your team. Make the team feel bad, and you'll have a low retention rate. So many owners don't even realize that they're doing this. They don't understand that they're being negative in front of their teams because it's natural—it relieves their feelings. Stay positive, especially in front of your team, because they are watching you, even when you don't think they are.

Show That You Care
About Your Employees

I spoke about caring for your employees to a group of 50+ convenience store owners and managers in Wausau, Wisconsin. It turned out that the owners also had a tire business attached to the stores. To show their care for their employees, who are lifting tires and moving them around all day, they hired a chiropractor to give adjustments to all the staff once a week.

You will retain more employees if you show that you care about them. On their birthday, every employee gets a choice between a birthday cake or pizza. Some say to me, "Since I became a teenager, you're the only dude, Alex, who's ever bought me a cake. Thanks so much, dude."

With this kind of incentivization, you can't pick and choose. If leaders pick and choose who gets the cake or pizza, it undermines the effectiveness of the incentives. Even the least capable employee should get the same as all the others. If the employee isn't very capable, and you don't feel that person deserves a cake or a pizza, let the employee go before his/her birthday comes around. Otherwise, you will undermine the feelings of your team as some employees feel left out.

Every employee gets gifts for their birthday. For the past few years, I've also bought them a turkey for Thanksgiving. This is partly personal: I love Thanksgiving more than any other holiday. So, I hand my staff members an uncooked turkey, and even the ones who are not from the U.S. appreciate the chance to enjoy the wonderful holiday of Thanksgiving. After all, they have to cook the uncooked turkey.

So, I tell them: "We're closed on Thanksgiving. Celebrate the holiday at home with your family."

The Importance of a High-Performance Culture Based on People

Managers, of course, need a different kind of incentive. Owners offer incentives linked to labor—does your labor fall in line? Some incentives are linked to cost control—do your costs fall in line?

But if you create a high-performance culture based around people, then managers take care of your business as if they were part-owners, even though they are not.

I do make a point for my managers to do monthly reviews with their staff. This is critical. Because your managers sometimes get hung up on day-to-day processes, they forget to connect with their employees. It's not a formal monthly review.

We insist that our managers spend at least 20 minutes a month one-on-one with every employee. It doesn't matter what shift they're on, they have to take the time to connect with each one. Ask them, are they happy? What are their aspirations? How do they want to grow? That connection between the manager and the front line is very important. Even when your organization is growing and there are more employees, the manager must still connect with each employee. If you don't do that, those who are left out will feel like they're not part of the organization.

This is a different type of incentive. If I demand 100% performance from my managers and my employees, they will not stay with me. Insisting on perfection simply demoralizes people, and they are going to quit. You can't expect a person who is just getting a salary every week or paid hourly to give you 100% all of the time. It's more than you have a right to expect unless they have equity in your business. It doesn't matter what business you are in. If they own a part of the business, one could expect more from them because they have much more to gain.

But, from salaried employees, I ask for 100% on operations and customer service execution, of course. But if they give me 90 to 95% effort on executing operations and customer service, then I'm a happy man. And I will see a higher rate of retention.

If all QSR/Retail businesses ran at 90 to 95% on operations and customer service, we'd have very prosperous businesses.

Building Confidence for Retention

How do you build confidence in individuals? How do you empower them?

It's simple: You give them very easy tasks to start out with, then you build on that with more tasks. Add skills on, layer by layer, with increasing complexity. In this way, they build confidence, feel good, and want to keep working for you.

Some managers make the mistake of bombarding a good worker with far too much information. Then, inevitably, the person fails. And then his confidence is weakened. And it doesn't feel good being there, on the job. And eventually, that person leaves.

It's a slow game. Build confidence slowly, and gradually the person will become very capable of everything you want him to do.

Finally, when a person does quit, ask yourself why. What did I do wrong? Analyze the various factors and see if you can't change your behavior so that the next new worker will stay for a longer period of time.

Remember, in some cases, it's not your fault. But in some cases, it just might be. Be aware of what happened and try to understand why.

CHAPTER SUMMARY

Retention depends greatly on the atmosphere in the store, and this is usually determined by the attitude of the owner or manager. An owner who cuts corners will have workers who cut corners—the result is a disaster.

But an owner who shows confidence and satisfaction with his workers builds confidence and positive feelings. Show that you care about your employees in every way you can. Give them a pizza or a birthday cake on their birthday. Give them a turkey for Thanksgiving or something similar on a holiday. For managers, stay close with monthly reviews and regular discussion—don't let them become complacent. Altogether, build confidence with praise, make employees feel good, and they will stay with you.

CHAPTER 5

PULLING IT ALL TOGETHER – TAKING OVER A STORE

We've seen how creating a culture of happy, motivated employees leads to success in QSR retail—and in retailing in general.

But all that is just theory; this is how it works in practice. This is how I took over a store and made it significantly more profitable within a year.

About 15 years ago, I took over a restaurant, whose performance had been mediocre for a long time. It required a major transformation to get the store on track, to teach staff how to perform better, and to build a positive culture that makes my stores successful.

We usually take over right after closing on a store, and in this case, that day was a

Wednesday. We don't want staff to learn about a takeover until it actually happens because they can get panicky or even leave. I took over this store, and I wanted to keep everyone I could.

I sat down with the manager and explained that she would not lose her job, that nobody should be losing their jobs. I told her, "Just please understand that we are going to do things more by the book operationally, with more attention to the basics, and I want you to be open and ready for change."

In QSR, one often finds that people aren't open to change. They don't like to feel like they're going backward, being forced to learn again. Yet, I must ask them to go backward before we can go forward.

So, I sat down with the manager and explained this, and it frightened her. She was concerned about being able to adapt. But I explained that I'm a very even keel type of manager, always calm, always trying to communicate. I warned her that this might irritate her. "Ask me a million and one questions," I said. "I will never get angry with you or blame you for asking a question.

"So what do you expect from me?" she asked. "I expect you to do the best that you can with the tools that I am giving you," I continued. "I will give you every tool you need to succeed, even if it means spending some money. I don't mind spending a few bucks if I can make your job easier."

She looked relieved. She knew that there were a lot of managers like her who didn't have the tools and whose bosses weren't about to spend any money they didn't have to.

She understood that we were going to go back to the basics and that I'd be sharing a lot of ideas with her. I was looking forward to hearing her ideas as well.

She seemed to find that a bit daunting but was ready to give it a try. (It's really important to gauge the person's reaction at this point. You have to communicate carefully and effectively with each staff member).

I assured her that we would start slowly and with just one area of operations at a time.

This gives the manager a chance to understand my management style, and only once that is understood, do I move on to the next steps. It's all about slowly getting this person on the same page.

It was a very slow process, starting from that moment with the manager: It took me three to four months to get the store on track.

But the manager slowly changed. She began to learn the tricks involved in motivating staff. She started to give staff members the attention they needed. She paid close attention to the hiring process. In the end, all of the workers who were there at the start wound up leaving. They couldn't adapt to the new working style; they'd been badly trained and subjected to a poor, negative culture that provided more blame than praise.

Once I begin working with staff, there is constant, good-humored pressure that I apply to keep people improving. It's not pressuring in the sense of saying 'do this, do that!' but rather constant observation and lots of praise accompanied by teaching. Some people simply get tired of this pressure to improve and achieve. Some people just aren't team players or don't want to change and never quite fit in.

Starting All Over

The manager and I wound up starting fresh. She had to buy into the culture. She had to learn how to write a thank you note to the employee who closed the store properly at the end of the working day. She had to learn to call that employee personally and tell him/her 'good job.'

Learning to build a culture of good feeling based on praise isn't easy for everyone. Many are used to blame as they have received it all of their lives. But, once they learn the new culture, they love it and they communicate that love to others.

And that's what happened at this store. The manager built a new staff based on a solid culture of good feeling. Customers recognized it and brought their friends. "Hey," they said at first, "this place is nice and clean." Then they noticed that staff was smiling at them and making them feel welcome. When the manager is doing the right things, the team is working together, and the solid culture is established, the store sells itself.

The store soon nearly doubled the sales from when I acquired it. This has worked every time

I acquired a new store, and it will work for you too.

Ironically, when I sold the store five years later, the manager and the staff stayed and worked for the new owner. But sales dropped by half. Why? Because the new owner didn't sustain the culture I'd built, and the manager couldn't maintain it in the face of that change. Stores tend to express the personality of the leader. The new owner also wouldn't spend the extra money to provide the necessary tools to make the staff's job more efficient and less stressful. He started to cut corners. And the manager, seeing this, also grew less energized and stopped making sure everything was done just right. And this communicated to the staff, who did the same. This shows how important maintaining the right kind of atmosphere is.

CHAPTER SUMMARY

This is the story of how I used all the techniques described in the book to turn around a store that had been mediocre. Even though I had to lose the entire staff at the start, helping the manager understand the importance of operations and culture made the difference. Together, we found great employees, built a good feeling culture, and the store's profit doubled.

MARKETING

Marketing is important to success in QSR retailing. While many brands have marketing departments for national advertising. I believe the personal touch is just as important.

For example, many owners make the mistake when they take over locations of putting up signs that say "UNDER NEW OWNERSHIP" or "GRAND OPENING" only a couple days after taking over.

This can be a critical mistake. Make sure you are operationally sound before you begin to market your restaurant. You don't want to disappoint customers with mediocre service before you have the training and culture up to snuff. That will spread the word around town right away that the new store isn't all that great.

First, get your team operating at its best level. This can be frustrating, as it can take from several weeks to six months, or even longer in some cases. Then, tell everyone to come to see how good you are with your marketing. And adapt your marketing with your own personal touch to the community you work in.

Get Your Rep on the Street

Find someone on your team that smiles and has good people skills. Have them hand out coupons up and down the street in your trade area. But keep track of what is working. I used to put numbers on the back of each coupon. For example, Lexus dealer 1, Ford Dealer 2, Dentist office 3. Putting those numbers on the back of coupons helped me analyze which businesses were motivated by coupons, so I didn't have to waste time with others. Keeping track helps you understand what is working. I also would use local trade area direct mail pieces, like Val-Pak or SuperCoups, and the post office. These are paid direct mail pieces that go to homes. Save those as well to pay attention to what is working.

Get a Better Return Than Average

Any business has to calculate the cost of customer acquisition to know if their marketing efforts are effective. According to Propeller, in retail, the cost of customer acquisition averages about $10.[13] This makes sense because customer spend is relatively low compared with, say, the travel industry, so spending too much on customer acquisition wouldn't be worthwhile.

Doing direct mail marketing can sometimes not be worth the cost.

Marketers will tell you that if you have a 3–5% return on coupons, you've been successful. This means that if I send out 100 direct mail coupons and I get five back, it's a success. That pretty much the industry standard. Not in my book. If I can't get 20% back, it's not worth doing. Track your coupons; this will also permit you to negotiate for a better deal when working out the cost with these direct mail companies. Find different direct mail marketing pieces for your trade area. Some might work better than others.

I also find large employers near me with parking lots where I can put coupons on windshields.

13 https://www.propellercrm.com/blog/customer-acquisition-cost, n.d.

We also do bounce-back coupons, which is effective. A customer walks in, orders, pays, and then you hand them a coupon for their next visit.

You have to have some type of incentive to offer customers to help change their behavior to purchase in your restaurant. For example, we have done daily specials: On Monday, Chicken Teriyaki, on Tuesday, Meatballs. We offer a sandwich special every day of the week. I love this strategy because it makes customers think about us on a daily basis. When a customer thinks about lunch or dinner, they remember to find out if we offer their favorite sandwich special of the day today. It may not be the right one on a given day, but the customer is keeping us in mind. They might decide to come in anyway. It helps us with awareness.

We market our catering very actively. It is probably one of the most important of all of our marketing focuses. We reach out to office buildings and offer them free platters. I believe you have to give in order to receive. Just expecting to take all the time never works. Show people what you have to offer. Giving food away to show what a great product you have is a very effective strategy. Give a little taste to medical offices, doctors' offices, or to large corporate buildings. Catering is more of a relationship business with a great product. You could have a great product but no relationship, you will have a difficult time getting catering orders. Your marketing must focus on building a relationship with the people and businesses around you.

Be part of your community by sponsoring Little League teams and joining Facebook groups. This is a particularly effective means of building your catering business, as well as a very useful way to find new employees: Keep both of those activities in mind as you reach people in the community via Facebook groups.

Let me share an example of something I recently did to help build catering sales. Fairfield University is right down the street from my stores. I hired a college student to work in my office and to send emails to assistant coaches of teams that were coming in to play against Fairfield University. Everything is public information. Find the assistant coaches email online of the team that is coming into town a week or two before they come to play your home team— could be baseball, soccer, football or any other sports activity with teams. Email them to let them know that you are offering a special discount for their team because they are coming into town.

Using this strategy has helped increase my catering sales by 300%.

By identifying areas of opportunity as I've described, you can make marketing a valuable tool to expand your business. But the strategy will only succeed if your team is executing the basics properly. You can't overcome a bad reputation with marketing, but you can easily spread the word about your good reputation if you have one.

CHAPTER SUMMARY

There are ways to market very effectively, and these are not always the ones the marketing experts suggest. Getting an employee out on the streets to hand out coupons is very effective—if the employee is smiling and personable. Giving customers bounce-back coupons is another way. For catering, giving out some free food to important locations is also very effective. Be part of your community; don't just rely on the national advertising. You also have to do something locally.

But no marketing will work if the operational basics aren't in place and if the team isn't integrated into a culture of good feeling. Achieve those two things, and they will bring customers back time and time again.

FINAL CHAPTER

A CALL TO ACTION

This final chapter distills down and simplifies the most important points from all the chapters. It is a call to action for you, as a business owner or manager, to improve your hiring and training practices, find new ways to motivate your staff, and create a winning culture that your employees can't help but want to be a part of.

Hiring

Remember to be out front before the candidate walks in, then implement the three-step interview process.

Step 1: Walk in the front door

Step 2: Walk to the interview table (nonverbal cues)

Step 3: Interview

Training

Communication is the key to training and staff interaction.

Find a good app to communicate with all of your staff. Also, remember to use short videos of two minutes or less and get to the point. Using your phone is perfect for training videos.

Motivation

For every negative, give two positives.

Know your people. Please don't be lazy in language. Understand that using keywords that are relatable will help motivate individuals. Each employee has unique life experience, so use different language and incentives to motivate them.

Retention

Be sincere about praising. Your staff knows the difference between sincerity and flattery. Be self-aware—understand how you are being perceived as a leader.

Purchase a birthday cake or pizza for your staff's birthday. Don't forget the turkey for Thanksgiving.

Put these practical tools to work at your QSR/retail location. You will see a significant improvement in the quality of your hires, in the care your workers put into operations, and in the perception of you as a leader. If I can leave you with anything, it would be the understanding that people matter and that will never change. I always keep the mindset that I am not a boss but a coach. When I made that shift, the dynamics of my company changed.

www.ingramcontent.com/pod-product-compliance
Lightning Source LLC
Chambersburg PA
CBHW020511030426
42337CB00011B/341